# I Know Why the Caged Bird Sings: A Guide for Book Clubs

KATHRYN COPE

# CONTENTS

# 1 - INTRODUCTION

## The Reading Room Book Group Guides

This is one of a series of guides designed to make your book group meetings more dynamic and engaging. Packed with information, the Reading Room Book Group Guides are an invaluable resource to ensure that your discussions never run dry.

How you choose to use the guides is entirely up to you. The 'Author Biography', 'Literary Context' and 'Historical Context' sections provide useful background information which may be interesting to share with your group at the beginning of your meeting. The all-important list of discussion questions, which will probably form the core of your meeting, can be found in Chapter 10. To support your responses to the discussion questions, you may find it helpful to refer to the 'Themes and Symbols' and 'Character' sections.

A plot synopsis is provided as an aide-memoire to recap on the finer points of the plot and clarify the precise sequence of events in the novel. There is also a quick quiz - a fun way to bring your discussion to a close. Finally, if this was a book that you particularly enjoyed, either as a group or as an individual, the guide concludes with a list of books similar in either style or subject matter.

Be warned, this guide contains spoilers. Please do not be tempted to read it before you have read the original book as plot surprises will be well and truly ruined.

# 2 – WHY READ *CAGED BIRD*?

*I Know Why the Caged Bird Sings* is the first of seven volumes of autobiography written by Maya Angelou. It is also, deservedly, the most popular and critically acclaimed of her memoirs. First published in 1969, it is set in the 1930s and 1940s and documents Maya Angelou's coming of age as a southern black girl, confronting loneliness, racism, sexism and violence. It reflects not only her personal story, but the collective experience of the African American community during that period in history.

Although it is an autobiography, *Caged Bird* is often compared with the novels *To Kill a Mocking Bird* by Harper Lee and *Invisible Man* by Ralph Ellison. This comparison is valid, not only because of the similar themes of the books (i.e. prejudice, racism and the search for identity) but also because Angelou's memoir presents itself in a format more commonly found in fiction. Angelou ingeniously employs all the most effective techniques of fiction writing to make her memoir come alive. Maya's vernacular voice is vibrant and likeable, the dialogue is fresh and snappy and her childhood recollections of sensory experiences (e.g. the taste of fried catfish and the fragrance of tinned pineapple syrup) place the reader immediately in the moment.

Maya's early life involves many painful experiences, including abandonment by her parents and most shockingly, her rape as an eight-year-old. Despite its brutal realities, the details of her life are told with a wit and wisdom which prevents the memoir from becoming unbearably harrowing. Angelou balances her subject matter beautifully, juxtaposing moments of despair with humour. Hilarious recollections such as "the incident" where Sister Monroe has to be prised off the visiting minister in church demonstrate that while Angelou has the deepest respect for her community, she is also able to laugh at its foibles. The tone of *Caged Bird* and its title, taken from a poem by African American poet, Paul Laurence

Dunbar, clearly convey Angelou's message. In spite of the racism and oppression that the black community are confronted with, they are a people of laughter, song and courage. Angelou's memoir is both a damning depiction of racism in its many forms and a joyful celebration of the black community's strength.

# 3 – MAYA ANGELOU

*I Know Why the Caged Bird Sings* covers only the first sixteen years of Maya Angelou's extraordinary life. It took six further volumes of autobiography for Angelou to adequately cover the rest.

Born Marguerite Ann Johnson on 4th April 1928 in St. Louis, she soon became 'Maya' thanks to her brother's preference for calling her "Mya Sister." When she was three years old, her parents divorced and she and Bailey were sent to live in the rural Southern town of Stamps, Arkansas with their paternal grandmother, Annie Henderson. They continued to be moved around for the rest of her childhood, from St. Louis, back to Stamps, then California and finally San Francisco. At the age of eight she was raped by her mother's boyfriend.

A high achiever academically, she excelled in literature and drama and won a scholarship to study dance and drama at San Francisco's Labor School. At 14, she took time out of her studies to become the first African American to be hired as a San Francisco streetcar conductor. At sixteen she became pregnant and gave birth to her son shortly after graduating.

Maya struggled to support herself and her son, taking a variety of jobs including waitressing and briefly even resorted to prostitution. She yearned for a career in the entertainment business and in 1954 she left her son in the care of her mother while she toured Europe for a year with a production of the opera, *Porgy and Bess*. At this point she also officially changed her name to Maya Angelou. She went on to study modern dance with Martha Graham and in 1957 recorded an album, 'Calypso Lady.'

In the late 1950s, Angelou moved to New York and joined the Harlem Writers' Guild where she met a number of influential African American authors including James Baldwin who became a close friend. She also joined the Civil Rights Movement after being influenced by the speeches of Civil Rights Leader, Martin Luther King Jr.

In 1960, she moved to Cairo, Egypt where she married a South African freedom fighter and edited an English-language newspaper. Her marriage was volatile due to cultural conflict and they separated.

The following year she moved to Ghana, where she taught at the University of Ghana's School of Music and Drama and wrote for *The African Review* and *The Ghanaian Times*. During her stay in Ghana she met Civil Rights campaigner Malcolm X and agreed to help him build his new Organisation of African American Unity. Shortly after her return to the United States in 1965, however, Malcolm X was assassinated. In 1968, Martin Luther King Jr. asked her to organise a Civil Rights march, but he too was murdered. The deaths of the two prominent Civil Rights Leaders had a profound effect on Angelou, particularly as Martin Luther King was killed on her birthday. She became deeply depressed and when approached by Random House to write her autobiography, at first refused. Ultimately, however, she was unable to resist Editor Robert Loomis' challenge to write an autobiography that read like a novel. With the support of James Baldwin, Angelou began work on *I Know Why the Caged Bird Sings* which was published in 1969 to international acclaim.

Maya Angelou continued her work as a Civil Rights activist throughout her life. Her strong voice and intelligence were officially recognised by three Presidents of the United States. Both Gerald Ford and Jimmy Carter appointed her onto Presidential committees. In 1993, at President Bill Clinton's request, she wrote and performed a poem 'On the Pulse of Morning', for his inauguration, making her one of only two poets in American history to receive this honour.

Angelou's work in the Arts spanned literature, film and theatre. Some of her many achievements included the Presidential Medal of Arts in 2000, the Lincoln Medal in 2008, three Grammy awards, Pulitzer Prize nominations, over 50 honorary degrees and an Emmy nomination for her appearance in the television adaptation of Alex Haley's *Roots*. She also became Reynolds Professor of American studies at Wake Forest University.

Maya Angelou died on May 28th, 2014, having achieved what would seem impossible. Aware of the limitations placed upon African American women from an early age, she refused to be confined by them and proved through her achievements that prejudice has no legitimate foundations.

# BIBLIOGRAPHY

## Autobiographies

*I Know Why the Caged Bird Sings*

*Gather Together in my Name*

*Singin' and Swingin' and Gettin' Merry Like Christmas*

*The Heart of a Woman*

*All God's Children Need Traveling Shoes*

*A Song Flung up to Heaven*

*Mom & Me & Mom*


## Other Non-Fiction

*Wouldn't Take Nothing for My Journey Now*

*Even the Stars Look Lonesome*

*Phenomenal Woman*

*Letter to My Daughter*

*Hallelujah! The Welcome Table*


## Poetry Collections

*Just Give Me a Cool Drink of Water 'Fore I Diiie*

*Oh Pray My Wings Are Gonna Fit Me Well*

*And Still I Rise*

*Shaker, Why Don't You Sing?*

*I Shall Not Be Moved*

*On the Pulse of Morning*

*A Brave and Startling Truth*

*Amazing Peace*

*Mother*

*Celebrations*

## Children's Books

*My Painted House, My Friendly Chicken, and Me*

*Kofi and his Magic*

*Now Sheba Sings the Song*

*Life Doesn't Frighten Me*

# 4 – LITERARY CONTEXT

## AUTOBIOGRAPHY

*I Know Why the Caged Bird Sings* is generally classified as an autobiography as it is a non-fictional account of a significant period of the author's life. Like many traditional autobiographies, it is narrated in the first person, events are related in a chronological order, and the narrative drive focuses on the development of the author from her beginnings to the person she later became.

Readers familiar with the autobiographical genre, however, will immediately notice that *Caged Bird* is very different stylistically to the average autobiography. Angelou's memoir reads like a novel, which was exactly her intention. When first approached to write her memoirs by Robert Loomis of Random House, Angelou was unenthusiastic. When he dared her to write an autobiography as if it were fiction, however, she rose to the challenge.

In *Caged Bird*, Angelou pushes the boundaries of autobiography, introducing elements more commonly found in fiction such as dialogue, characterisation and sensory details. These embellishments give the narrative a more vivid and immediate feel than would generally be found in a conventional autobiography. Angelou also creates a childlike voice for her younger self, intervening occasionally with her authorial adult voice to comment on incidents with the benefit of hindsight. Most controversial of all, Angelou admitted that she sometimes amended the truth to improve her story (e.g. she blended the characteristics of three or four people to make one more interesting character).

By blending autobiography with the techniques of fiction, Angelou highlights some of the ambiguities of the genre as a whole. Autobiographies sell themselves as a true representation of a life, but even the most conventional examples of the genre raise questions about how possible it is to write 'the truth'. As memoirs are generally written in the later stages of life (Angelou was 40 when she wrote *Caged Bird*), they depend upon the reliability of memory. They also involve an apparently objective interpretation of events – something very few of us would be capable of achieving! Finally all autobiographies involve the selection of the most interesting and pertinent material as, if an author included a blow-by-blow account of their life it would make for extremely tedious reading. Just as Angelou quite openly chooses only key moments from her childhood to fit in with her themes, all memoirs involve a certain amount of editing and shaping which we would normally associate with the crafting of a novel. In *Caged Bird*, the crafting process is simply more pronounced.

# BILDUNGSROMAN

In *Caged Bird*, Angelou also draws on the classic tradition of the bildungsroman. Particularly popular in the nineteenth century, the bildungsroman focuses on character development, tracing the psychological growth of its protagonist. Often beginning with an emotional loss or trauma, the story follows the main character's journey from childhood to adulthood as they go in search of answers to life's questions. Buffeted by the slings and arrows of life, they pass from innocence to experience; their final goal being self- knowledge and emotional maturity.

Charlotte Brontë's *Jane Eyre*, Mark Twain's *The Adventures of Huckleberry Finn*, and any number of Charles Dickens' works (*David Copperfield*, *Great Expectations*, *Oliver Twist* …) are all classic examples of the bildungsroman.

Angelou subverts this generally very traditional and 'white' genre to relate the specific details of her own painful journey. In sharing this history, she also expresses the collective trials experienced by adolescent African American girls in a racist, sexist society.

Like many bildungsroman protagonists, Maya is parentless and displaced when the story begins. The narrative follows her beginnings from feeling abandoned and ugly to discovering her strengths and a sense of belonging. Her journey is often painful, with her rape as the nadir of her sufferings, but by the end of the novel, her trials have made her stronger and she has come to a greater understanding of herself.

# AFRICAN AMERICAN LITERATURE

Although Angelou draws on literary genres previously dominated by white writers, *Caged Bird* also uses and develops traditional African American forms of expression.

One of the earliest forms of black American literature was the slave narrative that emerged in the nineteenth century. These were memoirs written by former slaves describing their trials under the oppression of slavery and their eventual escape to freedom. Angelou uses a similar trajectory in *Caged Bird*, describing the crushing effects of a racist society upon her as a girl and then sharing her journey towards freedom and empowerment. The easy, vernacular style of her writing also pays tribute to the African American oral tradition, as storytelling was a vital way for non-literate blacks to pass down their culture and histories.

The influence of later African American writers involved in the Civil Rights Movement is also evident in Angelou's writing. From the turn of the twentieth century onwards, the focus of black American writing shifted. Slavery had come to an end but black Americans were now allocated a 'free but not equal' status within American society. African American writers began to explore the wider themes of racism, segregation and inequality, strongly influenced by the American Civil Rights Movement of the 40s, 50s and 60s. Just as black activists fought to end segregation and racism and create a sense of black nationalism, authors addressed the same issues in their writing. Perhaps the most famous novels emerging from this period are *Native Son* by Richard Wright and Ralph Ellison's *Invisible Man*. Both address the African American man's sense of alienation and struggle for acceptance in American society. Even more influential on Angelou, however, was author, James Baldwin, who became her friend and mentor. As Baldwin was a homosexual black man, his work addressed both race and sexuality. In his novels and short stories he described just how it felt to be black and homosexual when neither of those identities was considered acceptable in American society.

*Caged Bird* made an important contribution towards the canon of black American literature, as it expressed the black woman's voice within the Civil Rights Movement. While James Baldwin highlighted the particular prejudices faced by black homosexual men, Angelou outlined the double prejudices faced by black women. Through portraying her own personal journey towards activism against racism, Angelou also demonstrated the important role women played in the Civil Rights Movement.

Angelou's memoir paved the way for other African American women writers who succeeded in bringing black literature into the mainstream from the 1970s onwards. Many of the themes she touched upon in *Caged Bird* were revisited in fiction by black women authors. In her novel, *The Bluest Eye*, Toni Morrison explores in depth the devastating consequences of imposed white perceptions of beauty already touched upon in *Caged Bird*. Likewise, Alice Walker's *The Color Purple*, focuses upon sexual abuse as one of the many forms of oppression that black women may face. Both Walker and Morrison went on to win the Pulitzer Prize for their fiction, and Morrison became the first African American to win the Nobel Prize for literature. These literary honours firmly established African American women's writing as a legitimate and important genre of American literature.

# 5 – HISTORICAL CONTEXT

## THE JIM CROW ERA

The Jim Crow Era is the term used to describe the status of African Americans in the USA between 1877 and the mid-1960s. Although slavery had come to an end, the 'Jim Crow Laws' were put in place to ensure that African Americans remained second-class citizens. The laws dictated strict racial segregation in the Southern states of the USA, including the prohibition of mixed marriage. They also mandated the segregation of all public facilities (e.g. toilets, restaurants, schools, workplaces and public transport).

While black Americans were officially allocated a "separate but equal" status, in reality this segregation led to economic, educational and social disadvantages for black people. In *Caged Bird*, this is demonstrated in the graduation speech by Edward Donleavy which clearly highlights the academic advantages which pupils in white schools benefited from. It is also shown in the incident where the white dentist refuses to treat Maya, forcing Momma to travel some distance to take her granddaughter to see a black dentist.

The enforced segregation of the Jim Crow Laws only served to fuel racist attitudes in the South. Violence erupted and black communities were terrorised by white racist organisations such as the Ku Klux Klan.

Although segregation largely applied to the Southern United States, it was also practised to some degree in the North. African Americans were excluded from applying for certain types of housing and particular jobs. Maya's fight to become the first black streetcar conductor in San Francisco illustrates this point.

# THE GREAT DEPRESSION

The period of economic recession known as the Great Depression began in 1929. The USA experienced a decade of poverty and high levels of unemployment.

One of the most severely injured industries was agriculture, largely based in the South. As both rural blacks and whites suffered from decreased incomes from farming, racial tensions increased during this period. The right of black farmers to make a living was undermined by whites who resented their entitlement to property, animals and even wages. This is illustrated when Maya observes how difficult it is for the cotton pickers of Stamps to make a living wage, no matter how hard they work.

The economic situation caused by the Great Depression led to the 'Great Migration', when a significant number of black people left the South to settle in Northern cities where they were offered work in factories and other industrial sectors. The impact of this is described by Maya when she goes to live in San Francisco. The long-term effect of the Great Migration was to create a new sense of independence within the black community. The American Civil Rights Movement was created as black activists fought to end segregation and racism.

# THE CIVIL RIGHTS MOVEMENT

The American Civil Rights Movement was particularly active during the 1950s and 60s. Its aim was to end racial segregation and discrimination against black Americans and achieve constitutional voting rights. Activists conveyed their message through non-violent campaigns of civil resistance, including sit-ins, boycotts and marches. As a result, a number of Civil Rights Acts were passed, including a 1964 Act banning racial discrimination in employment practices, and the 1965 Voting Rights Act that restored and protected voting rights.

Martin Luther King Jr. was one of the major leaders of the movement, urging non-violent resistance to racism. Malcolm X also emerged as a more militant Civil Rights figurehead, striving for black nationalism rather than multiculturalism. Both leaders were famously assassinated in 1968 and 1965 respectively.

# 6 - THEMES & SYMBOLS

## DISPLACEMENT

At the beginning of *Caged Bird*, Maya's sense of displacement is demonstrated when she recites that she is not there "to stay." The phrase becomes her defence mechanism as she is sent to live in seven different homes during her childhood. It is a personal reminder to herself not to become too settled, as nothing can be relied upon as stable or permanent.

Maya and Bailey's sense of rootlessness is exacerbated when they first receive Christmas presents from their parents. Having previously assumed that they were orphans, the children have to face the reality that they have been willingly abandoned by their mother and father. Although their parents re-enter their lives later on, their presence is always somewhat sporadic and unpredictable. Maya is unable to bond with her biological father, whilst Bailey becomes excessively attached to his beautiful mother. Angelou demonstrates how their feelings of abandonment as children lead to them searching for affection in other inappropriate places. Bailey's longing for his mother leads to his ill-fated sexual relationship with an older girl, Joyce, whilst Maya's desire for physical affection from a father figure leads her to confuse Mr Freeman's sexual assaults with love.

The personal displacement of Maya and her brother is also representative of the wider displacement of the black community by the African diaspora. Beginning with slavery, when Africans were taken from their homelands and taken to strange countries, this displacement continued after Emancipation in the United States, as the black community struggled to make a living in a racist society. As it became increasingly difficult to survive in the rural South, black workers migrated to the Northern cities for work. Maya finds herself most at home in San Francisco, where many black people have relocated, as this is a city which seems to embody displacement.

# RACISM

In *Caged Bird*, Maya Angelou successfully captures the racist attitudes prevalent during the 'Jim Crow era.' Particularly in the South, African Americans were clearly relegated to the position of second-class citizens and Maya soon begins to appreciate how segregation and racism influence every part of a black person's life.

Growing up in the strictly segregated rural community of Stamps, Maya has virtually no experience of white people and struggles to even believe that they exist. Despite the absence of white people, however, the oppressive nature of white society is still keenly felt.

Although they are 'free men', rather than slaves, the black agricultural workers struggle to earn enough to survive. The threat of white violence continually hovers over the community. Black men live in fear of the accusation of sleeping with or raping white women (the consequence of which Bailey sees when he is forced to drag a murdered black man out of a lake). Visits from lynch mobs and the Ku Klux Klan are also a constant possibility, leading to Uncle Willie's uncomfortable night hidden in the potato bin. Angelou demonstrates how distrust of whites influences the mindset of the community. Momma rarely speaks about white people for fear that even the most inoffensive comment could prove dangerous if it were overheard.

As Maya gets older, she begins to experience more personal incidents of racism. She recounts her white employer's attempt to rename her, the demoralising speech at her eighth grade graduation and the white dentist's hypocritical refusal to treat her.

Angelou depicts many different forms of resistance to racism in her memoir. Momma is aware of the dangers of active resistance and so her stance is subtle but not passive. She takes the moral high ground and maintains her dignity in the face of disrespectful taunting by white girls. She also derives satisfaction from the thought of white people burning in hell and takes revenge on the white dentist by charging him interest on a loan. Daddy Clidell's friends are more audacious, deliberately using the prejudiced views of white people to defraud them.

Collective resistance of racism is shown in the episode where the community of Stamps come together in the Store to listen to Joe Louis's world championship boxing match. Louis's win is shown to be a symbolic victory for the entire black community, proving that they are not inferior to whites. Sadly, the incident also demonstrates just how desperate the black community are for vindication. Maya realises that the hopes of the entire African American people are centred upon the sporting success of one black man.

Maya assimilates the different types of resistance that she sees and begins to perform her own acts of defiance. She begins with the relatively small gesture of breaking Mrs Cullinan's china and goes on to fight racist hiring policies, refusing to give in until she lands the landmark role of first black streetcar conductor in San Francisco.

# GENDER

As an adolescent black girl, Maya finds herself faced with triple obstacles: male prejudice, racism and black powerlessness. The nadir of Maya's suffering under these three burdens is her rape by Mr Freeman. His sexual assault on her is an expression of his own feelings of impotence in society as a black man. Raping Maya is one of the few opportunities he has to assert his power. The way black women often take the brunt of black male frustration is also demonstrated in the relationship between Big Bailey and Dolores.

Throughout her childhood, Maya becomes close to a number of exceptionally strong female role models. Momma is an astute businesswoman and morally strong, Vivian is tough and independent, Grandmother Baxter is the formidable head of her explosive family, and Bertha Flowers is educated and cultured. Maya comes to admire these women as they have carved their own path in life and do not rely upon men financially or for their sense of identity. She comes to realise that their remarkable strength comes from surviving and triumphing over the sexism and racism that black women inevitably face. It is this triumph over adversity that the title of Angelou's novel expresses. Like her female role models, Maya is caged by racism and sexism but nevertheless refuses to be cowed and continues to sing.

# RELIGION

In depicting the devoutly Christian community of Stamps, Angelou highlights the role religion plays in providing comfort to the black community. For Momma, her faith provides moral guidance, enabling her to maintain a sense of dignity and self-righteousness during trying times.

The description of the annual revival meeting demonstrates that the church also offered open resistance against racism. The preacher delivers a sermon denouncing false charity, clearly targeted at white Christian hypocrisy. He also promises divine justice and revenge, implying that black people are beloved by God due to their oppression, whilst white people will be punished for their prejudice. Maya notes how the congregation are buoyed up by this sermon, taking comfort in the idea that they are God's chosen people. The feeling is short-lived, however, as they soon fall silent when they pass a rowdy honky-tonk party on the way home. The revelry of the party reminds them that sin is not the sole preserve of the white world and that their place in heaven may not be entirely secure after all.

Maya's attitude to religion is ambivalent. She acknowledges the value of Momma's strict moral code and endeavours to be a good person as she grows up. Angelou comes to see the comfort religion offers the black community as a double-edged sword. Although it can provide inner strength in times of need, the message that justice will be done in the next life may encourage black people to endure racism in the present, rather than fight it.

# ETHICS

When Maya goes to live with the Baxter family and later when she is introduced to Daddy Clidell's friends, she comes to question some of her previously held beliefs about what is ethical. She realises that intelligent black men craving success have very few legal avenues to follow. Daddy Clidell's conmen friends make a living from swindling bigoted whites and Maya finds that she cannot condemn them as they are simply trying to turn round the unfair standards of racist society in their favour. Maya calls this the "ethics of necessity."

# NAMING

The importance of naming is a recurring theme in *Caged Bird*. Names have a special significance in the African American community as they are tied up with notions of identity and freedom.

Negative generic names such as 'nigger' and other derogatory derivations have been used throughout history to dehumanise blacks and justify their subjugation. Also, on an individual basis, one of the many things taken away from slaves, along with their freedom were the names given to them at birth. The allocation of a new name, combined with the adoption of the slaveholder's surname was standard practice and signified that as slaves, they were possessions rather than human beings. Angelou demonstrates how this insidious re-naming process continued after the abolition of slavery when employers would often decide on new names for their servants. In *Caged Bird*, Maya is initially prepared to dismiss it as a mistake when her employer, Mrs Cullinan, mispronounces Marguerite as Margaret. When Mrs Cullinan deliberately starts calling her Mary for the sake of convenience, she is not prepared to passively accept it, as the black cook, Glory, has already done. Maya instinctively understands that the casual re-naming is a misuse of power and a subtle attempt to erase her identity. She breaks Mrs Cullinan's china; her first conscious act of resistance against racism.

Maya's real name is Marguerite Ann Johnson and she is called 'Ritie' by most of her family. The fact that she chooses to go by the name of Maya Angelou as an adult and writer is an assertion of her freewill and independence. The name Maya springs from Bailey's nickname for her when they are children: "Mya Sister." Her choice of this as a name for life indicates the depth of love between them.

Other characters in *Caged Bird* acquire the names they are most commonly known by through merit. Grandmother Henderson, who becomes Maya's only reliable source of stability quickly becomes 'Momma' as she is the most consistently maternal figure in their lives. Similarly, although Vivian's second husband is not Maya's biological father, he becomes 'Daddy Clidell' as he is a positive paternal figure, while her unreliable real father remains Big Bailey.

# BEAUTY

Angelou begins *Caged Bird* with a description of her humiliating experience of reciting a poem in front of the church congregation for the Easter service. The source of Maya's self-consciousness is her physical appearance. She has eagerly anticipated the day, fantasising that the lavender taffeta dress Momma has altered for her will transform her into a beautiful white, blonde girl. When she puts the dress on, however, she realises that she is still, in her own eyes, an ugly, ungainly black girl.

Maya equates beauty with whiteness as she has already internalised society's message that to be black is to be inferior in every respect. The way the black community have come to accept this message is demonstrated when Maya receives her first present from her mother: a doll with yellow hair and blue eyes. It is also highlighted by the fact that Maya's male contemporaries are sexually interested only in the lighter skinned girls with straight hair. Dark-skinned Maya is forced to proposition a boy to experience her first fully consenting sexual encounter.

Angelou ridicules white standards of beauty in the scene where Bailey and Maya go to the movie theatre together. Maya is horrified at the 'comic' black stereotyping in the movie but consoled by the fact that the white movie star, whom the audience adore, looks just like their mother, only less beautiful. When Maya tears the stuffing out of the blonde blue-eyed doll her mother sends, it turns out to be a symbolic act. As she grows in confidence, Maya is to learn that true beauty lies within.

# LITERATURE

Maya discovers her love of literature early in her childhood and it is to prove a huge comfort to her, providing an escape from life when she struggles to cope.

Maya's thirst for books and learning leads to her gradual understanding that freedom and literacy are intimately related. After Mr Freeman's murder, Maya refuses to talk, convinced that the lie she told in court as good as killed him. Maya's later relationship with Mrs Flowers demonstrates, however, that words can be empowering as well as destructive. Through reciting poetry aloud to Mrs Flowers, Maya reclaims her voice and begins to appreciate that the older lady respects her for her fine mind. It is ultimately this intellect which will lead her to accomplish so much in later life.

Despite her love of literature, Angelou points out that her reading material was generally limited to white male-centred fiction. Her first love is William Shakespeare but she considers reading his work a guilty pleasure, as he was a white Englishman. Similarly, Maya escapes into adventure stories, but the protagonists are always male, leading her to wish that she were a boy. In later life, Angelou was to take huge steps in addressing the lack of black female representation in literature by writing of her own experience.

# FAMILY

Getting to know her family is an important part of Maya's development. During her time in Stamps, Momma and Bailey are the only family Maya knows and she defines herself only through them. Both are to remain pivotal figures in her life, but with the reappearance of Vivian and Big Bailey, Maya comes to learn a great deal more about who she is and where she comes from. Although her mother's side of the family, the Baxters, are a violent clan, Maya admires the strong bond they have with one another. It is from her Baxter uncles that she hears stories about her forgotten early childhood experiences, including the origin of her nickname. The discovery of her family is therefore also a journey of self-discovery.

Angelou makes it clear, however, that the bonds she chooses to make beyond her blood relatives are an equally important part of who she becomes. Maya essentially rejects her biological father, Big Bailey, instead choosing to think of the caring yet strong Daddy Clidell as her father. Her friendship with Louise Kendricks is also important, as this is the first relationship she builds entirely outside of her family's influence, demonstrating an assertion of independence from them.

## MOTHERHOOD

Angelou explores different types of mothering through her depiction of Momma Henderson and Vivian Baxter. Momma fulfils the role of classic black matriarch, ensuring that her grandchildren are well cared for, clean and respectful whilst maintaining strict discipline. She is also selfless, sending the children away when she fears racial tension is becoming too dangerous in the South. By contrast, Vivian is not a typical maternal figure. Independent and spontaneous, she clearly loves Maya and Bailey but places the arrangement of her own life above the needs of her children.

Both Vivian and Momma are crucial figures in Maya's childhood and she comes to admire the different strengths of both of them. The memoir comes full circle when Maya transforms from abandoned child into a mother herself. It ends with Vivian teaching Maya to trust her maternal instincts and significantly the memoir itself is dedicated to Angelou's son, Guy.

# 7 - LOCATIONS

Location holds a great deal of significance to Maya in *Caged Bird*. The continual process of relocating plays a large part in Maya's sense of displacement and alienation. How she reacts and adapts to the contrasting locations she is confronted with often expresses her state of mind. Maya's observation of how the black community respond to racism in each of these locations also provides an overview of the African American experience across America.

## Stamps, Arkansas

Maya sees the full impact of the Jim Crow Laws when she lives in Stamps in the rural South. Here, racial segregation is so complete that she struggles to even believe that white people exist. Their presence is still felt, however, in the fear of the community. Momma does not dare speak out against white people as she is afraid of the consequences and the town lives under the continual threat of attacks from white lynch mobs and the Ku Klux Klan. As a result, Maya comes to think of white people with a mixture of horror and revulsion.

Here, the economic effects of segregation also become evident to Maya as she observes the physical and financial hardships that black farm workers have to endure.

While Maya lives in Stamps, the Store is the centre of her world. It is also the heart of the town; a place where the locals come to socialise, commiserate and rejoice with one another. Despite, or perhaps because of the hardships that they suffer, the people of Stamps form a strong and cohesive community.

## St. Louis

St. Louis could not be more different from the rural Southern backwater of Stamps. When Maya first arrives, she decides she will never become accustomed to the traffic, noise and completely different pace of life. True to her vow, she never settles here, correctly assuming that before too long she will have to move on.

While living with the Baxters, Maya is treated to a very different view of race relations. Although racism is still prevalent in St. Louis, the Baxters display none of the fear of white people that is so tangible in Stamps. Maya is astounded to learn that her uncles fearlessly fight black and white men alike. She also notes that her mother's family live very differently from the devout, hardworking community of Stamps, making their living in less conventional ways and casually breaking the law. Completely self-sufficient, the Baxter family are fiercely loyal to one another but do not feel the need to be part of the wider black community.

## San Francisco

Moving to San Francisco is a turning point in Maya's life. After the upheaval of World War II, it is a city which seems to embody change and displacement. Maya finds herself one of many displaced people as the population of San Francisco is continually in flux. Its former Japanese residents have been removed to internment camps during the war and replaced by both black and white factory workers relocated from the rural South.

Here, schools are unsegregated and blacks and whites work side-by-side in the factories. Maya realises, however, that this does not mean that the city is a harmonious melting-pot. Racial tension still exists as rural whites bring their racist attitudes with them, whilst rural blacks still fear and distrust white people. The fate of the former Japanese residents is also a reminder that racial minorities are always expendable. Blacks who move here do so in the uncomfortable knowledge that job opportunities have been created by the persecution of a different ethnic minority.

Ironically, the feeling that almost everyone is an alien in San Francisco provides Maya with a sense of belonging for the first time. She finds a positive father figure in Daddy Clidell, whose friends introduce her to a bold scheme of resistance against racism in which they use the prejudices of white people to con money from them. Maya begins to blossom and realises that active resistance to racism is important to her. Her new found confidence gives her the strength to fight for the position of first black conductor on the San Francisco streetcars.

# 8 - PLOT SYNOPSIS

## Prologue

The setting is Stamps, Arkansas on Easter Sunday in the early 1930s. Marguerite (otherwise known as Maya), stands before the congregation of the Methodist Episcopal Church. The lavender taffeta dress she had hoped would transform her into a pretty blonde white girl has not had the desired effect: she is still a large, plain African American girl. Maya struggles to remember the words of the poem she is reciting and is overcome by the urge to visit the bathroom. She flees down the aisle but is tripped up by one of the other children. Humiliated, she loses control of her bladder and runs from the church laughing and crying at the same time.

## Chapter 1

Maya is three years old and her brother, Bailey, is four. Their parents have just divorced and they are put on a train from California to Stamps, Arkansas. Although their father has paid a porter to accompany them, he abandons them in Arizona, leaving the children to complete the journey alone. Around their necks are paper signs stating their final destination.

When they arrive in the Southern, rural town of Stamps, the children live with their paternal grandmother, Annie Henderson and their Uncle Willie. Mrs Henderson (or Momma as they come to call her) is a respected member of the community who owns and runs the only store in the segregated black area of Stamps. The Store is the social and business heart of the black community.

Maya comes to appreciate the harsh reality of life for the average black Southern citizen when she observes the black cotton labourers who come into the Store during picking season. She notices that in the morning, the workers appear optimistic but after a day of toiling on the plantations they are exhausted and earn barely enough to live on. The author notes that this is when she came to despise the stereotype of cheery "song-singing" cotton pickers.

## Chapter 2

Maya describes how Uncle Willie, who was crippled in a childhood accident, becomes a strict but effective teacher to her and Bailey. Willie is the target of jokes and resentment from the rest of the community as, despite his handicap, he lives a more comfortable life than most thanks to the business acumen of his mother. One day, when she is five, Maya catches Willie trying to conceal his disability from a couple of strangers who have called in to the store. Maya sympathises with Willie, understanding that he must be tired of being labelled as handicapped by others.

Maya has discovered a love of reading, and suffers a certain amount of guilt over her passion for William Shakespeare as he was a white man.

## Chapter 3

Mr Steward, the white ex-sheriff of Stamps, warns Momma that the Ku Klux Klan is expected to pay a visit to the area as a black man has been accused of "messing with" a white woman. As Willie is a likely scapegoat, they hide him in the potato bins. The Klan does not pay them a visit, but Maya can hear Willie's moaning from the bins all night.

## Chapter 4

Maya describes the stark contrast between her and Bailey. While she lacks confidence and considers her kinky hair and dark skin to be ugly, her brother is charming and universally agreed to be handsome. Maya does not resent Bailey for his physical advantages and considers him to be the most important person in her world. The bond between them is extremely strong and Bailey uses his wit to defend his sister, insulting those who rudely comment on her plainness.

Maya recalls how, as racial segregation was so complete in Stamps, she did not encounter white people, but thought of them with a mixture of fear and revulsion.

## Chapter 5

Momma impresses two important maxims upon Maya and Bailey: cleanliness is next to godliness and children should respect their elders. Maya observes that everybody in the community respects their elders apart from the "powhitetrash" children. One morning, when Maya is ten years old, three poor white children approach the Store. Maya reluctantly obeys when Momma sends her inside but watches her grandmother's encounter with the girls. She seethes with rage when she sees the girls mock Momma whilst her grandmother hums hymns and fails to retaliate. The encounter ends when the oldest girl performs a handstand, revealing her lack of underwear. Momma politely says goodbye to the girls as they leave. Maya is furious, believing the girls have humiliated Momma. When she sees Momma's serene face, however, she realises that her grandmother has scored a moral victory over the white girls by maintaining her dignity.

## Chapter 6

Maya recalls how she and Bailey dreaded visits from the Reverend Howard Thomas, the church elder of the district. The obese Reverend would stay with them every three months, eating all the best parts of their Sunday dinner. By eavesdropping on conversations between the Reverend and Uncle Willie, Maya and Bailey learn about the castration and murder of a black man who had allegedly done "it" with a white woman.

One Sunday, while he is delivering a sermon, Reverend Thomas is overpowered by a notoriously over-enthusiastic worshipper, Sister Monroe. His false teeth are knocked out and Bailey and Maya receive a whipping from Uncle Willie for laughing uncontrollably.

## Chapter 7

Maya pays tribute to Momma's power and strength. She explains that her grandmother was a "realist" in terms of race relations believing it was dangerous for black people to even talk to whites, let alone show open defiance. She did, however, once allow a black man accused of assaulting a white woman to take refuge in her store. Momma became respected and revered amongst the black community for the incident after the man was later apprehended. When the accused testified that he had taken refuge with her, the judge subpoenaed "Mrs Henderson" only to realise he had mistakenly referred to a black woman as 'Mrs' (a title usually reserved for white women).

## Chapter 8

Maya describes the delayed effect of the Great Depression upon Stamps. As the owners of the cotton fields dropped wages, poorer families became increasingly dependent upon welfare agencies. Momma still manages to keep the Store going, introducing an exchange system for customers with no money.

One Christmas, Maya and Bailey are confused to receive gifts from their parents in California. Both had convinced themselves that their parents were dead. They cry, wondering what they did wrong to make their parents send them away. Maya and Bailey tear the stuffing out of the blonde, blue-eyed doll their mother sent but decide to keep the tea set intact, just in case their mother ever returns.

## Chapter 9

When Maya is seven, her father, Big Bailey, arrives in Stamps unexpectedly. A large handsome man, he is out of place in Stamps as he owns a car and speaks like a white man. He stays for three weeks before announcing that he is going to take Maya and Bailey to St. Louis to see their mother. Momma appears saddened but accepting of their departure. Maya feels uneasy in her father's presence and still regards him as a stranger. Bailey is delighted to spend time with Big Bailey, however and father and son begin to bond.

When they arrive in St. Louis and finally meet their mother, Vivian, the children are overwhelmed by her beauty. Bailey falls in love with Vivian and Maya notes that her brother and mother are alike in both physical appearance and personality. A few days later, Big Bailey leaves for California.

## Chapter 10

In St. Louis, Maya and Bailey live in the home of their grandparents and rarely see their mother. Grandmother Baxter is a formidable, "nearly white" woman with connections to both the criminal underworld and the police department. As a result, the children meet an interesting collection of people who make a living from organised crime.

Vivian's three brothers all have city jobs and explosive tempers. Despite their love of inflicting violence on outsiders, however, they are fiercely loyal to one another and Maya appreciates their strong family bond. She also gains some knowledge of her own history, as the Baxters tell them stories about their childhood before they were sent to Stamps. Maya learns that she acquired her nickname when Bailey insisted on calling her "Mya Sister" instead of Marguerite. Tommy is Maya's favourite uncle. He helps to boost Maya's self-esteem by reassuring her that lack of physical charms is unimportant, as she is clever; a far more valuable asset. This is proven when Maya and Bailey start school in St. Louis and find they are far more advanced than the other children.

After six months, Maya and Bailey move in with Vivian and her boyfriend, Mr Freeman.


## Chapter 11

Disrupted by yet another relocation, Maya has nightmares and Bailey has developed a stutter.

Vivian and Mr Freeman have different working patterns as she works in a gambling parlour at night and he is a foreman. Maya feels sorry for Mr Freeman as whenever Vivian is absent he spends his time pining for her to return.

Maya begins sleeping in her mother's bed due to her nightmares. One morning, Maya awakes to find Vivian has already risen and Mr Freeman is sexually molesting her whilst masturbating. Afterwards he threatens to kill Bailey if Maya tells anyone what happened. Maya isn't sure exactly what has happened but as she has been starved of physical affection, she enjoyed Mr Freeman holding her close. What she cannot understand is what she has done to make her mother's boyfriend angry. Maya keeps the secret and Mr Freeman avoids her in the following weeks. Missing the physical closeness she experienced with Mr Freeman, Maya sits on his knee. Again he molests her.

Maya begins spending her Saturdays at the library and the world of books becomes more real to her than her own life.


## Chapter 12

One Saturday, when they are alone together, Mr Freeman rapes eight-year-old Maya. He threatens to kill her if she screams and to kill Bailey if she tells anyone. Following her ordeal Maya passes out from the pain.

When she comes round, Mr Freeman tells her to go to the library as she normally would. Maya attempts to obey him, but intense pain forces her to return home. She goes to bed, hiding her bloodied drawers under the mattress.

When Vivian finds Maya in bed, she is sympathetic, suggesting she may be coming down with measles. Later the same night, Maya hears her mother and Mr Freeman arguing.

In the morning, Vivian tells Maya that Mr Freeman has moved out. Maya remains feverish and in pain and believes that she is dying. When Bailey changes her bed linen her bloody drawers fall out from under the mattress at Vivian's feet.

## Chapter 13

Maya is taken to hospital where Bailey urges her to name her attacker. When Maya reveals the rapist was Mr Freeman, he is promptly arrested.

In court, Maya is asked whether Mr Freeman ever touched her inappropriately prior to the rape. Fearing that she will appear guilty and that her family will reject her if she tells the truth, she says no. Mr Freeman is sentenced to one year and one day in prison.

Later that evening, a policeman visits Grandmother Baxter to inform her that Mr Freeman had been temporarily released from custody and his body has been found behind the slaughterhouse. He had been beaten to death. Grandmother Baxter appears unsurprised at the news and tells Maya and Bailey never to speak of Mr Freeman again.

Maya is convinced that the lie she told in court is directly responsible for Mr Freeman's death. Believing that her words have the power to kill, she resolves to stop speaking to everyone except Bailey and maintains her silence for weeks. At first the Baxter family accepts her muteness as a sign of post-rape trauma but as time goes on they become angry and start beating her. Eventually, she and Bailey are sent back to Stamps. Bailey is devastated and Maya feels guilty, unsure if Momma sent for them or if the rest of the family grew tired of her.

## Chapter 14

Maya is relieved to return to the uneventful world of Stamps but remains withdrawn and speaks very little. Bailey is frustrated as he misses his mother and St. Louis and becomes uncharacteristically sarcastic with the unwitting people of Stamps.

## Chapter 15

Mrs Bertha Flowers, a refined black gentlewoman, takes Maya under her wing. Aware that she is intelligent but silent in the classroom, Mrs Flowers invites Maya to her home and lends her some books on the condition that they are read aloud. She also asks Maya to memorise a poem to recite when she next sees her.

Maya returns home excitedly with cookies for Bailey only to be whipped by Momma for using the phrase "by the way", which Momma interprets as blasphemous.

## Chapter 16

When Maya is ten she begins working as a housemaid for a white woman, Mrs Viola Cullinan. Maya feels sorry for her employer when she learns that she is infertile and that her husband has had two beautiful daughters by a black woman. She works extra hard to try to make amends and excuses the fact that the white woman mispronounces her name as Margaret.

One day one of Mrs Cullinan's friends suggests that Maya should answer to the name of Mary for the sake of convenience. When Mrs Cullinan takes her friend's advice, Maya is furious. She deliberately becomes slapdash in her duties in the hope of getting fired, without success. On Bailey's advice, Maya drops her employer's favourite heirloom china, making it appear to be an accident. Mrs Cullinan rages at Maya, calling her a "clumsy nigger". When Mrs Cullinan's friends rush over, attracted by the furore, one of them enquires if the culprit is Mary. Mrs Cullinan screams that Maya's name is Margaret and throws a piece of crockery at Maya.

## Chapter 17

One evening Bailey goes to the cinema but has still not returned well after dark. Momma takes Maya with her to search for him and they meet him on his way home. He fails to offer an explanation for his whereabouts and receives a whipping from Uncle Willie.

For several days afterwards, Bailey is withdrawn. He finally explains to Maya that the movie he went to see starred a white actress, Kay Francis, who looked just like their mother. He had stayed late to watch the movie a second time.

The next time a Kay Francis movie shows at the theatre, Maya accompanies Bailey to see it. She notes the white people in the theatre laughing at the degrading Negro stereotypes depicted in the film. Maya has the last laugh, however, as the white actress the audience idolise looks just like her black mother, only less beautiful.

Bailey is sad when they come out of the theatre and frightens Maya on the way home by running across the railway tracks in front of an oncoming railway car. The incident leads Maya to worry whether Bailey may one day board one of the trains and leave her. A year later, Bailey fulfils her prophesy by jumping on a box car, but only gets as far as Baton Rouge, where he is stranded for two weeks.

## Chapter 18

The black community of Stamps gather together for the annual revival meeting. The preacher delivers a sermon condemning false charity. Although he does not mention white people, the entire congregation are aware that the preacher is attacking hypocritical white Christians who give to poor blacks with the expectation of excessive gratitude. The sermon dwells on the divine justice that will be wreaked upon those sinners who practise false charity.

At the end of the meeting, the worshippers are visibly buoyed up by their renewed sense of righteousness. Their elation does not last, however, as on the way home, they pass a 'good-time' premises blaring out music, reminding them of the more sinful side of their world. Maya observes that whilst one is perceived to be sinful, both the honky-tonk party and the revival meeting briefly raise the spirits of the poor black community, providing the promise of escape from the harsh realities of day-to-day life.

## Chapter 19

The Store is packed with people who have come to listen to the heavyweight championship boxing match on the radio. Joe Louis, a black hero, is defending his title and Maya explains how the pride of the black community is invested in the result of the match. If Louis loses, his defeat will appear to prove the white racist assumption that black people are inferior. When Louis wins, the people in the crowded store are elated, as to them it signifies that blacks are the most powerful people in the world.

## Chapter 20

During the annual summer picnic fish fry, Maya makes her first friendship with Louise Kendricks, a girl of the same age. With Louise, Maya learns the innocent pleasures of play and laughter for the first time in her childhood.

At school, Maya receives a note from an eighth grader, Tommy Valdon, asking her to be his Valentine. Maya shows it to Louise who explains that Valentine means love. Maya is frightened at the thought, as it reminds her of her experience with Mr Freeman and tears up the note. In class, for Valentine's Day, Maya's teacher reads cards sent by the eighth graders. Tommy has sent another letter to Maya saying that although he knows she tore up his note, he still considers her his Valentine. Maya is persuaded by Tommy's sincere tone and decides to make it clear that she returns his interest. When she sees him again, however, it is clear that he has already moved on.

## Chapter 21

Eleven-year-old Bailey constructs a 'Captain Marvel hideaway' in the yard and begins imitating sexual intercourse with girls inside the tent. During these naïve games, Bailey plays the father, the girl plays the mother and Maya plays the baby who sits outside to keep watch. Although the girls lift their dresses up, all participants stay fully clothed and virginal. Bailey loses his virginity to Joyce, a buxom older girl who takes the game several steps further. He becomes besotted with the advanced older girl and begins stealing food from the Store for her.

After a few months Joyce disappears and Bailey loses all interest in life. Maya discovers that Joyce ran away with a railroad porter and is furious with her for breaking Bailey's heart.

## Chapter 22

One stormy night, George Taylor comes to the Store. Mr Taylor is still broken-hearted at the loss of his wife, Florida, who died six months previously. Momma and Uncle Willie feed and comfort Mr Taylor who tells them that his dead wife appeared to him the night before declaring that she wanted children. Maya becomes frightened when Mr Taylor insists that the visitation was real and adds that his wife was accompanied by a laughing white baby angel. She remembers Mrs Taylor's funeral, during which she had her first glimpse of mortality when she viewed Florida Taylor's body in her coffin.

## Chapter 23

Maya is twelve years old and graduating from eighth grade. Like the rest of the community, she anticipates the graduation ceremony with excitement, particularly as her academic work was amongst the best in her year. Maya is now more comfortable in her own skin and has confidence in her abilities.

The mood of the graduation ceremony is ruined by a white guest speaker, Edward Donleavy. He tells the audience that as part of school improvements, the white school of the district has received new science and art equipment and assures them that their own school will soon benefit from improvements to their sports facilities and workshops. He also lauds the several great athletes who have graduated from their school. Maya notes that Donleavy's 'encouraging' speech only serves to highlight the limited number of options that are seen as viable for black people. His emphasis upon sport and practical skills rules out any consideration of the fact that the children at the school may be academically talented.

Henry Reed, one of Maya's classmates, follows the white speaker with a positive, well-delivered valedictory speech, but it fails to dispel Maya's gloom. When he leads the graduation class in the uplifting anthem 'Lift Ev'ry Voice and Sing,' however, Maya absorbs the lyrics for the very first time and feels proud of her black heritage. The transformative effect of the song brings home to her just how powerful poetry and music can be.

## Chapter 24

Maya is suffering from unbearable toothache. As the nearest black dental practice is 25 miles away, Momma takes Maya to Dr Lincoln, a white dentist in town. During the Great Depression, Momma loaned money to Dr Lincoln and intends to call in the favour.

When they arrive, Dr Lincoln refuses to look at Maya, stating that he does not treat black patients. Momma reminds him that her loan saved his practice. Dr Lincoln replies that he repaid the loan in full and he would rather stick his hand in a dog's mouth than a black mouth. Momma tells Maya to wait outside and goes into Dr Lincoln's office. Maya imagines Momma humiliating Dr Lincoln and forbidding him to ever work in the area again. Afterwards Momma takes Maya to the black dentist in Texarkana.

Maya later overhears Momma telling Uncle Willie that she made Dr Lincoln pay ten dollars interest on his loan. She acknowledges that it is a sin to ask for retrospective interest but felt that he deserved it. Maya decides she prefers her own imaginative version of events.

## Chapter 25

One day, Bailey returns to the Store visibly shaken and asks why white people hate black people so much. On the way home, he saw a dead black man being dragged out of a pond. A white man ordered Bailey and some other black men to help load the rotting corpse into a wagon and then pretended he was going to lock them in with the dead body.

Shortly after the incident, Momma begins planning to take Bailey and Maya to live in California with their mother.

## Chapter 26

Momma lives in Los Angeles with Maya and Bailey while Vivien finds them a place to live. Maya is devastated when the time comes for Momma to return to Stamps. They move into a large house with Vivian, Grandmother Baxter and their uncles.

Maya and Bailey start to get to know Vivien properly for the first time. Fun loving and spontaneous, she is also brutally honest. She supports herself and her children by gambling and once shot her gambling partner for insulting her.

World War II begins as the USA declares war on Japan. Soon afterwards, Vivien marries Daddy Clidell, a successful businessman. The family move to San Francisco.

## Chapter 27

Maya describes the cultural change that occurs in San Francisco with the advent of World War II. The areas of the city previously populated by Japanese residents are overtaken by Southern blacks as the Japanese 'disappear'. Black workers replace the Japanese who are now imprisoned in US government camps. Maya observes that the black community never speak about the Japanese displacement as they are simply focused on their own advancement in a white racist society.

The atmosphere of constant flux and displacement in wartime San Francisco makes thirteen-year-old Maya feel at home for the first time. She notes, however, that the city is sadly not without racial prejudice.

## Chapter 28

On starting school in San Francisco, Maya is automatically put up two semesters due to her good grades but finds herself out of place amongst the streetwise girls of her age. She transfers to George Washington High School in a white district of the city where she is one of only three black students. Maya finds the experience intimidating as the other students are more educated and confident. The one redeeming feature is Miss Kirwin, one of

Maya's teachers, who has a passion for knowledge, does not indulge in favouritism and never treats Maya differently because she is black.

When she is 14, Maya is awarded a scholarship to the California Labor School where she studies dance and drama.


## Chapter 29

To Maya's surprise, she becomes increasingly attached to Daddy Clidell who is her first positive father figure. He is the owner of numerous apartment buildings and pool halls and introduces Maya to his conmen friends who make a living from taking advantage of the prejudices of whites and swindling them. Maya does not condemn the conmen as she has come to realise that the ethics of the black community are based upon necessity. She acknowledges that as black people start from a position of disadvantage, they are forced to use every opportunity they can to advance themselves in the world.


## Chapter 30

Maya is excited to receive an invitation from Big Bailey to spend the summer with him and his girlfriend Dolores in California. When she arrives, Maya is surprised to discover they live in a trailer park. Living with her father's girlfriend soon becomes uncomfortable as Dolores is obsessively prim and tidy, whilst Maya is naturally messy and clumsy. Big Bailey observes their mutual discomfort from the side-lines with obvious amusement.

Big Bailey is a chef and takes frequent solo trips to Mexico, supposedly to buy Mexican ingredients. One day he invites Maya to accompany him, much to Dolores' indignation. They drive across the border to a Mexican village where the residents greet him warmly.

Maya and her father take part in a fiesta but towards the end of the evening Maya cannot locate her father. Vulnerable and frightened, she sits in the car and waits for him. Eventually Big Bailey appears, so drunk that he passes out on the back seat of the car. Maya has never driven before but decides she must be capable of it and lurches her way back to the border. She successfully reaches the checkpoint but then has a minor accident involving another car. The guards and passengers from the other vehicle become agitated believing Maya's prostrate father is a dead body. Big Bailey regains consciousness and immediately settles the matter with a mixture of charm and bribery. He drives the rest of the way home. Maya is angry that he does not recognise the scale of her achievement in driving them back to the border.

## Chapter 31

Big Bailey and Dolores argue when they return to the trailer park. Maya overhears Dolores claim that Maya has come between them. Big Bailey dismisses her feelings and storms out. On hearing Dolores crying, Maya determines to do the right thing by attempting to comfort her. Dolores rebuffs the attempt at reconciliation and calls Maya's mother a whore. Maya slaps Dolores and in the following scuffle, she realises that she has been stabbed in the side with a pair of scissors. She runs bleeding from the trailer and locks herself in her father's car. Dolores follows her, screaming, and circles the car with a hammer.

Big Bailey returns and drives Maya away. She assumes he is taking her to hospital, but instead, he drives her to a friend's house where a woman dresses her wound. Afterwards, he drives Maya to the trailer of another friend where she spends the night. Big Bailey visits the following day and leaves some money promising to return later that evening. Maya does not want to face her father's friends and decides to leave. She feels she cannot return to Vivian however, as she is afraid of the violence that may ensue if her mother realises she has been stabbed.

## Chapter 32

Maya sleeps in a car in a junkyard. When she wakes up, a group of teenagers are outside the car. Maya discovers that they are a community of homeless teenagers, made up of blacks, whites and Mexicans. They tell her she can stay providing she follows the rules of the community which ban theft and dictate that all earnings are shared equally.

Maya stays for a month, during which she becomes comfortable with racial diversity and learns tolerance. Finally, she calls Vivian and asks her to pay her airfare to San Francisco. She says her goodbyes to the group and returns to her mother.

## Chapter 33

Maya observes that sixteen-year-old Bailey has become almost unrecognisable since she last saw him. He is still 'in love' with Vivian and has begun wearing flashy clothing and using street slang in an attempt to emulate his mother's group of friends. Maya looks on helplessly as Bailey and her mother engage in an Oedipal struggle. Events come to a head when Vivian demands Bailey stops seeing his white prostitute girlfriend and he defies her. Bailey moves out and Vivian arranges a job for him as a dining-car waiter on the Southern Pacific.

## Chapter 34

Maya becomes restless and decides to take a semester off from school and find a job. She sets her heart on becoming a streetcar conductor only to discover that the company do not hire black employees. For weeks she pesters the streetcar company until she finally becomes the first black person to work on the San Francisco streetcars.

When Maya returns to school she feels she can no longer identify with her classmates. Her recent experiences have given her a new maturity. Maya summarises the difficulties for all American black women during adolescence as they face sexism, racism and powerlessness. She asserts that, as a result, the black women who survive these conflicts turn into formidably strong characters.

## Chapter 35

Maya reads the lesbian novel, *The Well of Loneliness* by Radclyffe Hall and begins to worry she may be gay. She is confused about exactly what a lesbian is, believing that her lack of 'feminine traits', (deep voice, large feet and underdeveloped breasts), may be classic characteristics. Vivian tries to assure Maya that her body is perfectly normal but Maya decides she must have sex with a boy to decide one way or the other. Aware that her male peers are only interested in chasing the lighter-skinned girls, Maya resorts to frankly propositioning one of the handsome boys in her neighbourhood. He readily agrees but the resulting unromantic coupling does nothing to convince Maya that she is 'normal.' Three weeks later she realises that she is pregnant.

## Chapter 36

Maya is horrified by her unplanned pregnancy but accepts full responsibility for it. She writes to Bailey, who advises her to keep it a secret from Vivian as she may make her leave school before graduating. Maya takes his advice and successfully graduates before announcing her condition. She is now eight months pregnant. Vivian and Daddy Clidell accept the news with stoicism.

Maya gives birth to a son. She immediately falls in love with her baby but is afraid she may accidentally harm him. Vivian encourages Maya to sleep with the baby in her bed, despite Maya's fears that she will crush him. When she awakes the next morning, Vivian points out that the baby is fine and Maya has instinctively cradled her son in the crook of her arm to protect him. Vivian declares that this proves that she doesn't have to worry about being a good mother, as her heart will lead the way.

# 9 - CHARACTER ANALYSIS

## Marguerite Johnson/ Maya Angelou

Marguerite, or Maya, tells her story through two distinct voices: that of a child, recalling her experiences as if they have only just occurred and her adult authorial voice, which looks back on events with the benefit of hindsight.

At the very beginning of the novel, Maya recites a mantra that she is not there to "stay" before the humiliating incident when she flees from church, laughing and crying. Angelou chooses to begin her memoir with this incident as it sums up her sense of insecurity when she was a young girl. Maya feels self-conscious standing before the congregation as she believes that she is ugly. Her fantasy that the taffeta dress will transform her into her ideal of beauty: a white, blonde haired, blue-eyed girl, naturally fails to occur. She judges her dark skin, unruly hair and angular body to be unsightly and believes others will do the same.

This lack of self-worth is exacerbated by Maya's sense of abandonment and displacement. Sent from St. Louis to the rural South by her parents when she is three years old, she has been passed over to her Grandmother's care with no explanation. Her personal mantra is a defence mechanism she uses to prevent herself from feeling settled when she may be forced to move again at any time.

During her early formative years in Stamps, Arkansas, Maya comes face-to-face with the grim realities of racism in the American South. As well as the constant threat of raids by the Ku Klux Klan, she endures personal racist affronts such as Dr Lincoln's refusal to give her dental treatment and Mrs Cullinan's racial abuse when she breaks her heirloom china. Slowly, Maya becomes aware that whilst black men have much to fear from racism, black women face three obstacles: white prejudice, black powerlessness and sexism. In recounting her own personal experience of these obstacles, Angelou is also expressing the collective struggle of all African American women.

In addition to the hardships imposed by racism, Maya recounts further personal traumas which only add to her sense of displacement. With the unexpected appearance of her father, Big Bailey, she and her brother are again uprooted to St. Louis to live first with their maternal grandparents and then with their mother, Vivian, all of whom are strangers to them. Vivian's boyfriend, Mr Freeman, takes advantage of Maya's yearning for comfort, molesting and eventually raping her. The experience traumatises her both physically and emotionally. Maya's description of the damage Mr Freeman inflicts on her undeveloped eight-year-old body is truly horrific, as is her worry that she may have encouraged his behaviour. His conviction for the crime, however, leads to further inner conflict. Maya already feels guilty about lying in court and believes that her sin has had fatal consequences when Mr Freeman is murdered. Believing that her words have a terrible power, she elects to be mute, enraging the Baxter family who send her back to Stamps.

Despite the hardships faced by Maya, her story is one of gradual empowerment. Angelou's belief that the three-fold obstacles that African American women face lead them to become formidably strong characters is highlighted in her own self-development through the story.

The young Maya is influenced by a series of strong female role models whom she learns valuable lessons from. Momma Henderson teaches Maya the importance of dignity and morality and Maya's moral consciousness is strongly developed as a result (displayed in her reluctance to lie in court). Bertha Flowers demonstrates to Maya that it is possible for black women to be cultured and educated. Mrs Flowers nurtures Maya's passion for literature and helps her to appreciate that her sharp intelligence is a more valuable attribute than beauty. In Vivian's case, she imparts the importance of independence for women, giving Maya the courage to make brave choices about the direction she wants her life to take.

An important part of Maya's evolution as a character is her increasing desire to actively confront racism. We see Maya's first act of resistance when she punishes Mrs Cullinan for the racist practice of renaming her servants. Incensed at being called Mary, she breaks her employer's best-loved china. Later on in the novel, Maya makes a considerable strike against racist hiring practices by petitioning a streetcar company until she is made the first black conductor aboard a San Francisco streetcar.

Maya also learns not to let issues of race consume her, however. Whilst living in segregated Stamps, she thinks of white people with a mixture of fear and repulsion and perceives them as barely human. The time she spends living in the Californian junkyard alongside a mixture of races makes her more tolerant and appreciative of human diversity.

By the end of *Caged Bird*, Maya is an intriguing mix of worldliness and innocence. Although she has experienced and learned a great deal, she finds herself unexpectedly pregnant after a naïve sexual experiment to find out if she is a lesbian. At sixteen, she has undergone a lifetime of trauma and has become a mother, but remains childlike in many ways.

## Bailey Johnson, Jr.

Maya's older brother, Bailey, is the most important person in Maya's childhood. As they are continually moved from grandparents to parents and back again, the one thing they know they can always rely on is each other.

The sibling bond between Maya and Bailey is touching. Both are intelligent and old beyond their years. Bailey, however, has inherited his mother's good looks, is a natural sportsman and is viewed as something of a golden boy. To Maya's credit, she never resents the natural gifts bestowed upon her brother and, in return, Bailey uses his quick wit to defend Maya from unkind comments about her ungainly physical appearance.

Bailey's reunion with his mother, Vivian, is a significant turning point in his life. After his prolonged absence from her, he is on the brink of adolescence when he is reintroduced to Vivian. Overwhelmed by her beauty, Bailey literally falls in love with her, confusing his need for a mother with his burgeoning sexuality.

When he and Maya are sent back to Stamps after Maya's rape, Bailey is devastated by this second separation from his mother. He withdraws behind a mask of sarcasm and moodiness and moons after a white movie star who looks like Vivian. His depression briefly lifts when he is coaxed by an older girl, Joyce, into having a sexual relationship, but he is left broken-hearted when she abruptly leaves him for a railroad porter.

Maya is struck by the change in her brother when they once again move in with their mother, this time in San Francisco. She is surprised to see that Bailey has started wearing flashy clothes, is using street dialect and is dating a white prostitute. This drastic alteration in Bailey demonstrates the dearth of positive opportunities for young black men. With no positive male role models to draw on, Bailey imitates the kind of man he is accustomed to seeing his mother with. Ironically, Vivian will not tolerate his behaviour and in a show of manly independence, Bailey moves out at the age of 16. The final separation from his mother is a painful wrench for him but he has come to understand that he needs to move on. He and Vivian come to an understanding with each other and he takes a job on the Southern Pacific Railroad, signifying a fresh start.

Distance grows between Bailey and Maya as they reach adolescence and the differences in their life experience takes its toll. As they grow older, the essential differences in their attitudes to life become more obvious. Whilst Maya confronts and questions racism, persisting until she is given the streetcar conductor job, Bailey is more of a defeatist. He remains a loyal and considerate brother to Maya, however, providing thoughtful advice at key moments, such as after the rape and during Maya's secret pregnancy.

## Annie Henderson (Momma)

Maya and Bailey go to live with their paternal grandmother when they are three and four years old respectively. They soon call her "Momma", representing the fact that she raises them for most of their childhood and is the only constant in their lives. She always has her grandchildren's welfare at heart, taking them in at a moment's notice and selflessly sending them away from the South when she believes that race-related violence is becoming a serious threat to their safety.

Mrs Henderson is morally irreproachable and brings the children up in accordance with Christian values and strict rules. Although, at times, she appears overly strict with the children, the rules she insists that they conform to are designed to instil them with a sense of moral responsibility and self-respect. Although she dislikes public shows of affection and is physically undemonstrative with her grandchildren, her love for them is never in doubt.

Married three times, Mrs Henderson is respected by the black community as the only black owner of a store in the area. Her status is raised a rung higher when she is 'erroneously' referred to as "Mrs Henderson" by a white judge. Clearly a woman of considerable business acumen, she started the Store as a mobile lunch counter, building it up until it became the heart of the black community. Angelou describes how, even during the Depression, her grandmother kept the Store going by introducing an exchange system for customers who did not have money. Although Maya goes through a phase of feeling embarrassed by her grandmother's uneducated dialect, she later comes to realise that her grandmother embodies the "mother wit" which Mrs Flowers teaches her not to underestimate.

Mrs Henderson's conduct teaches Maya valuable lessons about racism. She is a "realist" regarding race relations in the South and is careful not to openly criticise white people as she knows that repercussions may follow. When three poor white girls taunt her, Maya is initially horrified to see her grandmother turn the other cheek and remain polite to them. In retrospect, however, Maya realises that by retaining her dignity and not acknowledging their taunts, Momma achieved a moral victory over the girls. In the later incident with Dr Lincoln, however, she is so incensed by the dentist's refusal to treat Maya that she gives up the moral high ground and charges him retrospective interest on a loan as punishment.

## Vivian Baxter

Maya and Bailey's mother is an intriguing character. We first see her through the eyes of Maya and Bailey, who are dumbstruck by her beauty. Bailey immediately falls in love with her and Maya comes to the conclusion that her mother must have sent them away as she was simply too beautiful to have children. Vivian's real reason for giving up her children for a significant chunk of their formative years is not explained, beyond the fact that she and Big Bailey divorce. It is clear from the outset, however, that she is an independent spirit who answers to nobody: a temperament ill-suited to full-time motherhood.

Although she has a nursing degree, Vivian earns most of her money from gambling or working in gambling parlours. Tough, proud and financially independent, she is a strong woman, like her own mother, Grandmother Baxter. In the first few months of living in St. Louis, the children rarely see her, although when they do, she springs spontaneous surprises on them, such as their post-midnight private party.

Throughout her relationship with her children, Vivian flits between inattentiveness and moments of great supportiveness and love. She often leaves the children to their own devices and does not consider Maya's vulnerability when leaving her alone for hours with Mr. Freeman. She also fails to teach Maya about her own body, leaving her confused over the difference between physical affection and inappropriate sexual behaviour. We never discover why she sends Mr. Freeman packing prior to discovering Maya's rape, but Vivian is caring and maternal with Maya when she believes her to be ill. Like the rest of the Baxter family, however, she proves unable to deal with Maya's post-rape silence and presumably plays a part in sending her back to Stamps.

Vivian is similarly unaware of the effect her wild and unconventional lifestyle has on Bailey. When he begins imitating Vivian's male acquaintances in his style of dress and by dating a prostitute, she is oblivious to the fact that he is trying to win her approval. Instead, she hypocritically criticises his lifestyle.

Vivian and Bailey's relationship becomes increasingly explosive until Bailey makes the painful decision to move out. As Maya grows older, however, Vivian seems to develop a stronger bond with her daughter and becomes far more supportive. She admires Maya's tenacity in fighting for the streetcar conductor job and encourages her to put her heart into everything she does. Similarly, when Maya becomes pregnant, Vivian is uncritical and teaches Maya to trust her maternal instincts.

## Big Bailey Johnson

Big Bailey is Maya and Bailey Jr.'s biological father. After being absent from his children's lives for years, he turns up unexpectedly in Stamps to take them to St. Louis. The unsophisticated rural community is impressed by Big Bailey's flashy car, clothes and pseudo-English accent. When we learn he is a hotel porter, however, it becomes clear that he has delusions of grandeur and is living beyond his means.

Whilst Bailey immediately takes to his handsome, charismatic father, Maya is left cold, unable to see him as anything more than a stranger. She gets to know him better when she stays with him and his girlfriend, Dolores, in their trailer in California. Although Big Bailey's invitation to Maya seems to imply that he wants to make amends for neglecting his daughter, he pays little attention to her when she arrives and actively enjoys the tension between Maya and Dolores. He treats his girlfriend with barely concealed contempt, allowing her to keep house for him, with no intention of ever marrying her.

Maya briefly feels closer to Big Bailey when he takes her on a day trip to Mexico. The Mexican villagers greet him warmly and Maya notes he appears in his element amongst them. The day is ruined, however, when her father becomes too drunk to drive home and Maya is forced to attempt the drive herself. He again displays his selfishness and preoccupation with appearances when Maya is stabbed by Dolores and he takes her to a friend's house rather than hospital to avoid unnecessary gossip.

In retrospect, Angelou understands that her father's pretensions are a symptom of the lack of opportunities for black men in the United States. His swagger conceals frustration that his horizons are so limited. His behaviour also highlights, however, that girlfriends, wives and children often bear the brunt of this frustration.

## Grandmother & Grandfather Baxter

When Maya and Bailey are sent from Stamps to live with the Baxter family, it is a complete culture shock for them. Vivian's mother, Grandmother Baxter, could not be more different from the morally upright Mrs. Henderson. Maya describes her as a "quadroon" or "octoroon" (one quarter or one eighth black) who speaks with a husky German accent. She is a powerful figure, heavily involved in organised crime, as well as having influence with the police. Maya learns that she once nearly beat a man to death with a policeman's baton after he cursed her. It is also implied that she is involved with the murder of Mr Freeman after his rape trial.

By contrast, Grandfather Baxter is a quiet character, devoted to his wife and happy to remain in her shadow.


## Uncles Tutti, Tommy and Ira Baxter

Vivian's brothers all have city jobs: a considerable achievement for Negro men. They also all possess explosive tempers and a predisposition for violence, frequently getting into fights with both black and white men. The most positive quality shared by the brothers is their fierce loyalty to one another. Family is everything to them and Maya begins to gain a sense of her own place within the family by listening to their conversations. Through them, she discovers the source of her nickname, Maya, which evolved from Bailey's possessive labelling of her as "Mya Sister" when he was little.

Tommy is Maya's favourite uncle. He wisely advises her not to worry about being plain, as her sharp brain is far more valuable.


## Willie Johnson

Willie is Momma's son, and Maya and Bailey's uncle. He is in his thirties when Maya and Bailey first go to live in Stamps and has lived his entire life with his mother due to his disability. Maya learns that he was injured in childhood when he was accidentally dropped by the woman who was minding him.

Maya's disabled uncle finds himself something of a scapegoat amongst the community of Stamps. His disability makes him the butt of jokes and insults. Resentment and jealousy are also directed towards him, as, thanks to Momma, he lives a relatively comfortable life, whilst many other able-bodied black men struggle to make a living. Maya recalls an incident where she catches Willie attempting to conceal his disability from a couple of strangers who have called in to the Store. She both pities and sympathises with Willie, understanding that he must be tired of being defined by his disability. Maya understands that, like black women, Willie bears a double burden of oppression.

Willie is a devout Christian. His strict discipline and readiness to give the children a whipping acts as an effective incentive for swift learning when he teaches them at home.

## Daddy Clidell

Daddy Clidell is Vivian's second husband. She marries him after the children come to live with her in California. After her experiences with Big Bailey and Mr Freeman, Maya is prepared for him to be yet another transient male figure in her life. Daddy Clidell earns Maya's love with his combination of strength and warm-heartedness. Other than Bailey, he is the first male figure to respect Maya for who she is and he is genuinely proud when people assume Maya is his biological daughter. As a result, Maya thinks of him as her true father.

Although he is a successful businessman who owns apartment buildings and pool halls, Daddy Clidell never succumbs to the posturing and preening characterised by Big Bailey. He is a black man who has found the balance between confidence and arrogance and does not suffer from an inferiority complex over his lack of formal education.

## Stonewall Jimmy, Just Black, Cool Clyde, Tight Coat, Spots & Red Leg

When Maya meets Daddy Clidell's conmen friends, she is surprised that they are audacious enough to defraud white people by using their prejudices against them. Maya does not condemn their criminal activities as she notes how their apparent lack of ethics springs from necessity. As the potential of black men (and women) is severely limited by a racist society, they are forced to use whatever leverage they can find to better themselves.

## Mr Freeman

Mr Freeman is Vivian's live-in boyfriend when Maya and Bailey join her in St. Louis. Maya pities Mr Freeman as he is clearly no match for the vivacious Vivian and he pines in her absence.

Mr Freeman takes advantage of eight-year-old Maya's naivety and craving for physical affection. He sexually molests her on several occasions, threatening that he will kill Bailey if she tells anyone. Maya is confused and hurt by the experiences as she craves physical affection but cannot understand why Mr Freeman appears angry with her. When he finally commits rape, Maya attempts to hide her injuries until her bloody underwear is discovered.

The rape leaves Maya in turmoil over issues of love and her own sexuality. She is also forced to compromise her truthful nature by telling a lie in court. When Mr. Freeman is murdered, presumably by one of the

Baxter family, Maya feels responsible for his fate and she is haunted by guilt.

## Mrs Bertha Flowers

Maya considers Mrs Flowers to be the "black aristocrat" of Stamps. The refined black gentlewoman reminds Maya of the white English women she has read about in novels. When Maya returns to Stamps after her rape, Mrs Flowers coaxes her out of her silence by providing access to books. She nurtures Maya's love of literature and self-esteem, making her realise that intelligence is something to be proud of. For Maya, Mrs Flowers is a significant role model as she proves that it is possible for black women to be well-educated and cultured. She remains the benchmark for what a person can be throughout Angelou's life.

Maya is puzzled by Momma's friendship with Bertha Flowers and embarrassed when her grandmother gives away her lack of education in her use of improper grammar and dialect. Mrs Flowers warns Maya against intellectual snobbery, however, declaring that uneducated people can be highly intelligent and telling her to listen to the wisdom of "mother wit."

## Mrs Viola Cullinan

Mrs Cullinan is a Southern white woman who employs Maya as a housemaid. She, at first, appears to be a relatively benevolent employer, despite mispronouncing Maya's full name, 'Marguerite' as 'Margaret.' Maya overlooks the mistake and feels sorry for Mrs Cullinan, particularly when she learns that, although her husband has two illegitimate black daughters, she cannot have children herself. It soon becomes apparent, however, that beneath her veneer of gentility, Mrs Cullinan is a racist. Maya is moved to perform her first act of resistance against racism when the white woman starts calling Maya 'Mary'. When Maya deliberately smashes her employer's best-loved china, Mrs Cullinan's mask slips altogether and she lets loose a stream of racist insults.

## Miss Glory

Glory is Mrs Cullinan's cook, and a descendant of the slaves once owned by the family. She advises Maya not to worry about being re-named Mary and confesses that her own name was originally Hallelujah before her mistress changed it to Glory. Glory's passive acceptance of her re-naming is a striking contrast to Maya's resistance. It demonstrates that although she is a 'free' black woman, she is almost as enslaved as her ancestors by racist attitudes.

## Mr Edward Donleavy

Mr Donleavy is the white speaker at Maya's eighth grade graduation ceremony. The speech he gives demonstrates a subtle but insidious form of racism. In commending the school for the black athletes it has produced, he makes it clear that black students are not expected to excel in academic subjects. The speech reminds the previously excited students of the restrictions imposed upon them by society and casts a shadow over the graduation.

## Henry Reed

Henry is one of Maya's peers in her eighth grade graduating class. He is academically gifted and gives the valedictorian speech following Edward Donleavy's depressing offering. When he leads the class in 'Lift Ev'ry Voice and Sing', popularly known as the black national anthem, he restores his fellow students' sense of hope. Maya experiences a surge of pride in her black heritage and the incident makes her appreciate the power of black poets and orators to inspire others.

## Dr Lincoln

Dr Lincoln is the white dentist Momma takes Maya to when she has toothache. Although Momma knows he generally only treats whites, she believes he will make an exception for her, as she lent him money to keep his practice going during the Great Depression. Lincoln shows his hypocrisy, however, when he makes it clear that although he was happy to borrow money from a black woman, he refuses to put his hand in a black child's mouth. His attitude demonstrates a common myth amongst racist whites that blacks were somehow insanitary or carried diseases. Although Momma is powerless to force Dr Lincoln to treat her grandchild, she wreaks her revenge by asking him to pay retrospective interest on his loan.

## Dolores Stockland

Dolores is the prissy girlfriend Big Bailey shares a trailer with in Los Angeles. When Maya is fifteen she spends the summer with them both, but is unable to get along with Dolores who is obsessively tidy and jealous. Although Maya attempts to be conciliatory, assuring Dolores that she did not intend to come between her and Big Bailey, events come to a head when Dolores calls Vivian a whore. Maya slaps her and Dolores responds by stabbing Maya with a pair of scissors.

Although Dolores is not a likeable character, she is provoked by Big Bailey's blatant lack of respect for her. There is something pitiful in her attempts to keep perfect house in a trailer for a man who continually reneges on his promise to marry her. For Maya, she is one example of black womanhood that she definitely does not want to emulate.

## Louise Kendricks

Louise is the same age as Maya and the first real friend she makes. Before meeting Louise, Maya's interaction has been almost entirely with Bailey and the world of adults. Meeting Louise is a significant turning point in Maya's life as in her company she is able to be carefree and escape her problems in play. It also marks an important stage in Maya's development as her choice of Louise as a friend is made outside the influence of her family and reflects who she is as an individual.

## Tommy Valdon

Tommy is the eighth grader who sends Maya a Valentine at school. Maya initially distrusts Tommy and tears up the Valentine as she has come to associate 'love' with Mr Freeman's molestation of her. When Tommy writes her a second letter, however, Maya comes to believe that his interest in her is sincere and attempts to flirt with him, collapsing into girlish giggles whenever he approaches. Although Tommy quickly loses interest, the episode demonstrates to Maya that, despite her rape, it may be possible to indulge in more innocent romances with boys of her own age group.

## Joyce

Joyce is Bailey's first love. Buxom and four years Bailey's senior, she quickly turns his games of 'Momma and Poppa' into full sexual intercourse when

Bailey is only eleven. Just as Mr Freeman preys upon Maya's need for physical comfort, Joyce takes advantage of Bailey's longing for his mother.

Joyce breaks Bailey's heart when she runs away with a railroad porter. Although Maya despises her for it, we recognise that Joyce's life options are extremely limited. Orphaned and living with her poverty-stricken widowed aunt, she too is seeking security and love.

## George Taylor

George Taylor is a resident of Stamps, devastated by the death of his wife, Florida. One stormy night, he calls on Momma and Willie at the Store, seeking comfort. Maya is terrified when he tells them he has seen a vision of his wife accompanied by a laughing white angel. The incident highlights the importance of spirituality (including ghost stories and folk lore) in the lives of the black community.

## Mrs Florida Taylor

Maya attends Florida Taylor's funeral as the old lady bequeaths her a brooch. Her glimpse of Mrs Taylor in her coffin brings Maya face-to-face with mortality for the first time.

## Miss Kirwin

When Maya is transferred to a white school in San Francisco, where she is one of only three black students, Miss Kirwin is the only person who treats her as an equal human being. Her teaching style is a model for equal opportunities, displaying no favouritism and treating each student the same, regardless of colour or ability.

## Reverend Howard Thomas

Reverend Howard Thomas is a church elder who visits Stamps every three months. To Maya and Bailey's disgust, he stays with Momma and Uncle Willie on these occasions, devouring the best parts of their Sunday dinner. Maya gleefully recalls one particular sermon he delivers, as he loses his false teeth when an over-enthusiastic member of the congregation hits him with her handbag.

Maya's description of the Reverend's humiliating experience is extremely funny and demonstrates that, unlike Momma, she does not revere people who are unworthy of it, simply because they hold respected office within the church. The figures Maya does come to look up to are chosen purely by merit.

## Mr McElroy

Mr McElroy lives in a large house next to the Store in Stamps. Maya comments that during her time in the rural South, he was the only Negro she had ever seen, other than the School Principal, to wear a suit. As a child, Maya's romantic imagination creates mystique around Mr McElroy as he is the only financially independent black man in Stamps. In later life, Maya realises that he was a perfectly ordinary man who sold medicine and tonics to the gullible.

# 10 - QUESTIONS FOR DISCUSSION

1/ What is the significance of the title, *I Know Why the Caged Bird Sings*?

2/ Discuss the opening scene of the book. Why does Angelou begin her memoir with this particular incident?

3/ Discuss Maya's relationship with Bailey. What are the similarities and differences between them? What are the things that begin to come between the siblings as they grow older?

4/ What is Maya's attitude towards religion in the novel? Does she see religious faith as helpful for the black community?

5/ What did you make of the character of Vivian? Is she a good mother in your opinion? Do you think there is any truth in Dolores' accusation that she is a prostitute?

6/ Which characters serve as positive role models for Maya? What does she learn from them?

7/ Discuss the incidents of racism Maya experiences. How does she react? How do the other black characters in the novel deal with racism?

8/ Discuss Angelou's portrayal of Bailey, Big Bailey and Daddy Clidell in *Caged Bird*. What limitations do they face as black men and how do they deal with them?

9/ Angelou contrasts Momma's moral rectitude with the criminal activities of the Baxter family and Daddy Clidell's conmen friends. Both are a response to their place within a racist society. Which reaction did you have the most sympathy with and why?

10/ Angelou claims that adolescence is particularly painful for black girls as they face the triple oppression of racism, black powerlessness and sexism. Discuss how these three factors impact on Maya.

11/ Maya and Bailey's sexuality becomes mixed up with their issues over parental abandonment. Discuss how this confusion presents itself.

12/ Words hold great power for Maya. Discuss this in relation to her period of muteness and her love of books.

13/ Discuss Maya's character development through the book. In what ways does she change? How does hardship shape her and make her stronger?

14/ How does *Caged Bird* compare with other autobiographies that you have read? Were there any striking differences, particularly in style and narrative voice? Did the narrative style make you feel more involved in the story or have the reverse effect?

15/ In interview, Maya Angelou admitted that she took certain liberties with the truth in her memoir (e.g. blending several characters into one to improve the characterisation). Does this bother you? Would an autobiography that didn't 'rearrange' the facts make for a boring read? Bearing in mind the subjectivity of memory, is it ever possible to produce an autobiography that is one hundred percent 'true'?

16/ In *Caged Bird*, Angelou points out the insidious way that ideals of beauty are associated with white characteristics, e.g. as a teenager, she notes that her male counterparts are only interested in the paler-skinned black girls with straight hair. Is this still a relevant issue today? Do black women feel pressured to appear more 'white'?

# 11 - QUICK QUIZ

## Questions

How many of the following trivia questions can you answer correctly? Answers can be found on page 59:-

Q1/ What prompts Maya and Bailey's parents to send their children to live in Stamps?

Q2/ Why is Marguerite known as Maya?

Q3/ Why does Momma hide Uncle Willie in the potato bin?

Q4/ Which white author does Maya fall guiltily in love with?

Q5/ What name does Mrs Cullinan try to get Maya to answer to?

Q6/ What does Maya do to get her own back on Mrs Cullinan?

Q7/ Why does Momma believe Dr Lincoln, the white dentist, will treat Maya?

Q8/ When Maya first sees Vivian she believes she understands why her mother could not look after her and Bailey as young children. What does she think the reason is?

Q9/ How is Mr Freeman's rape of Maya discovered?

Q10/ Why does Maya stop talking after Mr Freeman's trial?

Q11/ What does Tommy Valdon send to Maya?

Q12/ What does Maya do for the first time on the way back from Mexico.

Q13/ In which city does Maya feel most at home?

Q14/ What ground-breaking job does Maya fight for in San Francisco?

Q15/ Why does Maya ask one of the handsome brothers in her neighbourhood to have sex with her?

# Answers

A1/ They get divorced.

A2/ Her brother called her "Mya Sister" when they were little.

A3/ Because they are expecting a visit from the Ku Klux Klan.

A4/ William Shakespeare.

A5/ Mary.

A6/ Breaks her favourite china.

A7/ Because she loaned him money during the Great Depression.

A8/ Her mother is too beautiful to have children.

A9/ Bailey discovers Maya's bloody underwear under the mattress when he tries to change her bedding.

A10/ Because she believed the lie she told in court caused his murder.

A11/ A Valentine.

A12/ Drive a car.

A13/ San Francisco, as it is full of displaced people.

A14/ The first black streetcar conductor in San Francisco.

A15/ She believes a sexual encounter with a man will help her to decide if she is a lesbian.

# 12 - FURTHER READING

## Extraordinary Autobiographies

The second volume in Maya Angelou's autobiographies is well worth reading for those left wondering where her extraordinary life journey took her next.

The memoirs of Harriet Jacobs and Solomon Northrup are two of the most famous and thought-provoking accounts of the devastating day-to-day experience of being an African American slave.

By contrast, Jeanette Winterson's autobiography describes her experience as a white English girl growing up within a fanatically religious family. Like Angelou, Winterson relates her story as if it were fiction and her realisation that she is a lesbian also leads to a personal struggle for identity and freedom.

*Gather Together in my Name*, Maya Angelou

*Incidents in the Life of a Slave Girl*, Harriet Jacobs

*Twelve Years A Slave*, Solomon Northup

*Oranges Are Not the Only Fruit*, Jeanette Winterson

## African American Fiction (by Black Authors)

*Go Tell it on the Mountain*, James Baldwin

*Conception*, Kalisha Buckhanon

*Invisible Man*, Ralph Ellison

*Beloved*, Toni Morrison

*The Bluest Eye*, Toni Morrison

*Mama Day*, Gloria Naylor

*Their Eyes Were Watching God*, Zora Neale Hurston

*The Color Purple*, Alice Walker

*Native Son*, Richard Wright

## African American Fiction (by White Authors)

Although written by white authors, both these novels eloquently explore the inequalities faced by African Americans at crucial points in American history.

*The Invention of Wings* centres upon the lives of white abolitionist, Sarah Grimké and a black slave, Hetty. In comparing the two women's lives Monk Kidd draws parallels between the fight to end slavery and the fight for equal rights for women.

*The Help* tells the story of black maids working for white Southern families in the early 1960s. Its revelations about segregation and racial inequality during this period are shocking and thought-provoking.

*The Invention of Wings*, Sue Monk Kidd

*The Help*, Kathryn Stockett

## 1930s Great Depression

The following novels explore the devastating effect of the Great Depression upon American rural communities.

*Tobacco Road*, Erskine Caldwell

*The Grapes of Wrath*, John Steinbeck

*Of Mice and Men*, John Steinbeck

# Further Titles in The Reading Room series

*Frankenstein: A Guide for Book Clubs*

*Gone Girl: A Guide for Book Clubs*

*The Book Thief: A Guide for Book Clubs*

*The Fault in Our Stars: A Guide for Book Clubs*

*The Great Gatsby: A Guide for Book Clubs*

*The Goldfinch: A Guide for Book Clubs*

*The Guernsey Literary and Potato Peel Pie Society: A Guide for Book Clubs*

*The Husband's Secret: A Guide for Book Clubs*

*The Light Between Oceans: A Guide for Book Clubs*

*The Storied Life of A.J. Fikry: A Guide for Book Clubs*

# BIBLIOGRAPHY

Angelou, Maya. *I Know Why the Caged Bird Sings*, Hachette Digital, 2010

Bloom, Harold. *Maya Angelou*, Chelsea House Publishers, 2001

Dickson-Carr, Darryl. *The Columbia Guide to Contemporary African American Fiction*, Columbia University Press, 2005

# ABOUT THE AUTHOR

Kathryn Cope graduated in English Literature from Manchester University and obtained her masters from The University of York. She is a reviewer and author of The Reading Room Book Group Guides. She lives in the English Peak District with her husband and son. The Reading Room series covers a wide range of titles for book group discussion from F. Scott Fitzgerald's classic *The Great Gatsby* to Gillian Flynn's contemporary bestseller, *Gone Girl*.

21859073R00038

Made in the USA
San Bernardino, CA
09 June 2015